Maze Craze
Spooky Mazes

Maze Craze
Spooky Mazes

Don-Oliver Matthies

Sterling Publishing Co., Inc.
New York

Library of Congress Cataloging-in-Publication Data Available

10   9   8   7   6   5

Published in 2003 by Sterling Publishing Co., Inc.
387 Park Avenue South
New York, NY 10016
Originally published in Germany in 2002 under the title *Spuk im Geisterschloss* by Edition Bücherbär im Arena Verlag GmbH
Wurzburg, Germany
© 2002 by Arena Verlag GmbH
English translation © 2003 by Sterling Publishing Co., Inc.
Distributed in Canada by Sterling Publishing
^c/o Canadian Manda Group
165 Dufferin Street
Toronto, Ontario, M6K 3H6, Canada
Distributed in Great Britain and Europe by Chris Lloyd at Orca Book Services
Stanley House, Fleets Lane, Poole BH15 3AJ, England
Distributed in Australia by Capricorn Link (Australia) Pty. Ltd.
P.O. Box 704, Windsor, NSW 2756, Australia

Printed in China
All Rights Reserved

Sterling ISBN 1-4027-0604-9

For information about custom editions, special sales, premium and
corporate purchases, please contact Sterling Special Sales
Department at 800-805-5489 or specialsales@sterlingpub.com

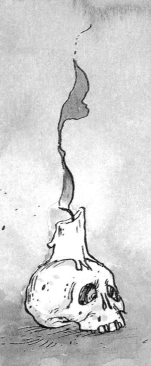

Draw a picture or place a
photograph of yourself here.

This book belongs to:

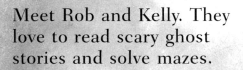

Meet Rob and Kelly. They
love to read scary ghost
stories and solve mazes.

Rob and Kelly are spending their vacation at their grandfather's old house in the mountains. Can you help them get through the winding roads and to the house?

start

end

In the evening, their grandfather reads a ghost story to the children. "On this very mountain there stood a haunted castle. Many say that the old cellar and vaults are still haunted."

As Rob and Kelly get ready for bed, they suddenly hear a faint noise. Rob checks under the rug and finds a secret trapdoor.

When they open the door they find a tunnel. "We better bring our flashlight along!" says Kelly. Can you show them how to go through the maze of pipes?

end

start

When they reach the bottom, they discover where the noise is coming from. A man is ringing bells and greets them. "In the next room Grimelda the Good Witch is waiting for you. But before you go, could you help me untangle the bell cords?"

When Rob and Kelly open the door they meet the witch. "Hello, I am Grimelda the Good Witch. The Evil Vampire has stolen my blue magic broom and I need it for the Flying Witch Race that takes place tonight at midnight. I think this maze on the wall will start you on your way. Can you help me?"

11

Rob and Kelly gladly agree to help Grimelda. Immediately, they set out on their search for the Evil Vampire. They enter Dr. Frankenstein's laboratory. He gives the children a key and tells them, "Find the Slimy Pond and open the door behind it with this key. But do you think you could help me with my maze experiments first?"

13

After Rob and Kelly help Dr. Frankenstein, they continue on their way. They suddenly come up to a hole in the ground. How can they get to the end?

Once they get out of the hole, Rob accidentally drops the key in a rat hole. How can the rat reach the key?

Finally they find Slimy Pond. The door, however, is all the way on the other side. What's the best way to get around the pond?

Rob and Kelly open the door with the key and find themselves in a dark cave filled with flying bats. Can you see where the bats perch?

17

"Not another room again!" sighs Kelly. "How are we going to get out of this one?" she asks Rob.

After they leave the room, they meet a skeleton rock band named "The Bones." "Do you know where the Evil Vampire is?" asks Rob. "Go next door," responds Fred. "There is a vampire party. Surely they will know where he is."

Nobody at the vampire party has seen the Evil Vampire. "Come and join us," they say to Rob and Kelly. "We are about to play a maze game and we could use your help."

start

20

end

end

Rob and Kelly keep following a path that seems to never end. As they cross a bridge, it begins to crumble. They are going to have to climb the walls, but how?

22

Now they have to go through some underground tunnels with rats running all around! The mazes on the wall will lead them through.

23

How can Rob and Kelly get past the small Crunching Critters and grab the key to the next room?

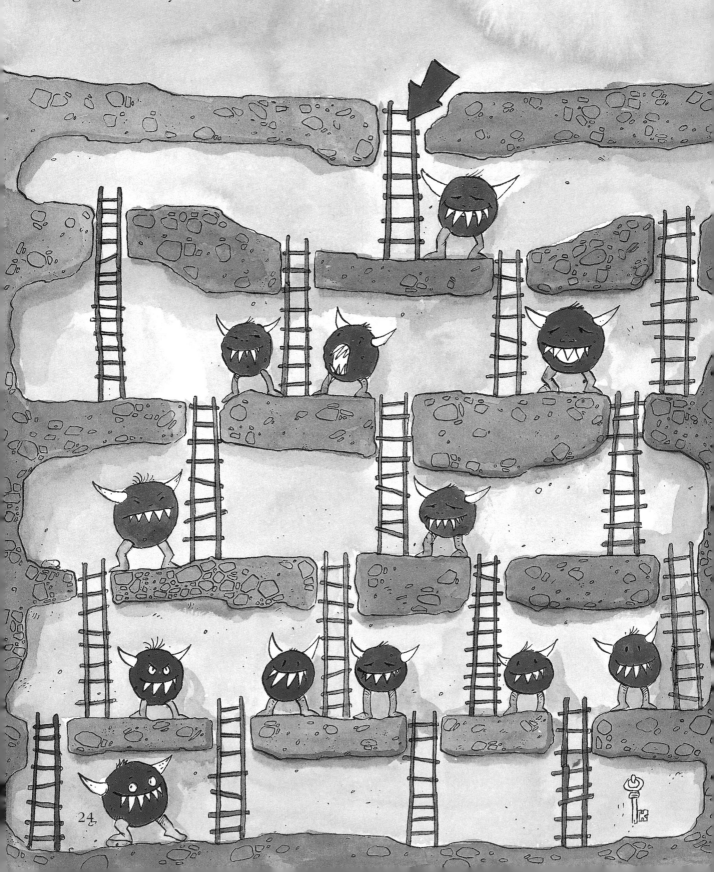

In the next room, the small Crunching Critters are ice-skating. Can you find the way to the end?

The children meet the Master of Magic Potions, who is casting a
ghost spell. Can you help them find their way through the ghosts?

Rob and Kelly begin to smell something. They open the door and find the cook. He tells them that the Evil Vampire hangs out in the room with an old throne. The cook explains to the children how he keeps the vampire away with garlic.

Rob and Kelly find the blue magic broom! But trying to reach it is extremely dangerous!

start

start

end

end

"Ha! You think you can just come in here and steal my beautiful broom?" the Evil Vampire yells. Luckily, the cook gave them some garlic and the vampire runs away.

Rob and Kelly return the blue magic broom to Grimelda. She can't wait to compete in the Flying Witch Race! Can you match the witches to their belongings?

Rob and Kelly say goodbye to all of their new friends. As a going away present, the friends give them one last maze to solve.

"Perhaps this vacation will not be so boring after all," says Rob. Kelly doesn't answer. She is already asleep and is dreaming of spooky mazes.

Answers

page 6

page 7

1=B
2=E
3=C
4=A
5=D

pages 12–13

A=1
B=5
C=2
D=3
E=4

page 14

page 15

page 16

page 17

1=E
2=B
3=D
4=D
5=A

page 18

page 19

1=John
2=Harry
3=Fred
4=Bill

pages 20–21

page 26

page 27

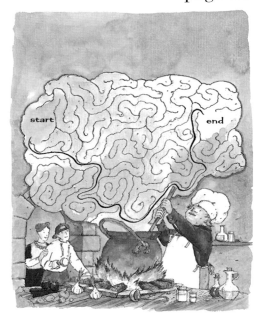

pages 28–29

The witch with the red broom
matches the horseshoe.
The witch with the white broom
matches the frog.
The witch with the blue broom
matches the magic potion.
The witch with the green broom
matches the magic hat.
The witch with the yellow broom
matches the magic wand.